CALLING FORTH THIS GENERATION

A 31 DAY JOURNEY
INTO PRAYING THE FATHER'S HEART

LINDA RACINE

Calling Forth This Generation
A 31 Day Journey into Praying the Father's Heart
By Linda Racine

Cover design and typesetting by Renee Evans (reneeevansdesign.com)

Printed in the United States

ISBN: 978-0-9966744-0-9

DEDICATION

This book is dedicated to my grandchildren Lucy and Sally Dannewitz, Samantha, Jack, James, Corena, Kaly, Sam and William Racine, as well as to all my spiritual grandchildren the Lord has privileged me to birth in His Kingdom. May my ceiling be your floor in your pursuit of the more of God. You are His delight and my joy.

ACKNOWLEDGEMENTS

Jesus Christ, You are acknowledged above all others for giving me my very life. You are my true inspiration and the only reason for this book.

Grandma Moody, you are still my heroine. Many years ago you introduced me to Jesus and set me on the path of friendship with the Holy Spirit. I will always love you and praise God for you.

My beloved husband Dick, words are inadequate to thank you for being a constant, living example to me of unconditional love, patience and encouragement. You are my treasure.

Pastors Dick & Jan Patterson, you have been a continual fountain of encouragement to my pursuing the more of God including the writing of this book. Thank you both.

Kimberly Schulz, you greatly encouraged me in volunteering your expertise and time to edit this manuscript. Thank you.

CONTENTS

INTRODUCTION

This devotional captures a glimpse of the Father's heart for this generation so the body of Christ, rising up as one voice, might partner in calling forth His heart's desire through prayer and declaration. It is not intended to be an end all, be all, but rather to fuel the flame of His passion within you to intercede for children and youth locally, across our nation, and throughout the world.

My own desperation for a move of God in our youth has been fueled by responses from many church leaders in the Bay Area saying, "Children are not a priority for us now," when approached about the possibility of a children's ministry taking place in their facility. It seems we are presently hearing and seeing a reflection of the disciples in Jesus' day who considered the children a "bother" and wanted to send them away. (Mark 10:13) But God's heart continues to resound, "Let the children come to Me. Don't stop them! For the Kingdom of God belongs to those who are like these children. I tell you the truth, anyone who doesn't receive the Kingdom of God like a child will never enter it." (Mark 10:14-15)

Repeated news reports of violence involving and taking out, even the youngest of our children; as well as conversations with teens and parents concerning destructive behavior in the lives of our youth, some of which has been enabled by overworked, overwhelmed and misguided parents, have further fueled my desperation.

So, in the quiet of the secret place, I cried out to Him, "Lord, it all looks so overwhelming to me; I don't know how to pray, or what to pray. What do **You** want me to do?" Then came a whisper from the All-knowing One who drew my heart to His, "Pray the children of the Bible." (Keep in mind that during Bible times anyone under the age of thirty could be considered a youth.) His response prompted further questions, which were followed by periods of abiding in His Presence and listening for His voice. What you hold in your hands is the result of what was heard as He began to reveal His unconditional love and plan for this generation. May this revelation encourage you to contend for the lives of the children and youth, calling them home to the heart of the Father.

Scriptures quoted herein have been taken from the New Living Translation (NLT) of the Bible unless otherwise noted. You are encouraged to read the prayers and declarations aloud so that His Words wash over you, raising your level of expectation as you call sons and daughters of God into their destiny.

CHILDREN OF PROMISE

Issac

Genesis 15-18 and 21

The Lord God promised Abram his descendants would be as numerous as the stars in the sky. However, as year after year passed, and Sarai, his wife did not become pregnant, what once seemed remote now looked impossible. So Abram and Sarai took matters into their own hands; Abram slept with Sarai's Egyptian maid Hagar. As a result, Ishmael was born; however, he was not the son God had promised. When Abram was 99 years of age, God appeared to him again and told him, "I will multiply you exceedingly. You will be a father of many nations," (Gen. 17:2, 4 NKJV) and God changed his name to Abraham. God also changed Sarai's name to Sarah meaning *princess of a multitude*. Say the names out loud. Abram, Abraham. Sarai, Sarah. Hear the breath of God as you speak Abraham and Sarah? The breath of God carries with it life.

Again God promised Abraham and Sarah a son saying, "I will return to you about this time next year, and your wife, Sarah, will have a son." (Gen. 18:10) In the fullness of time, the promised son, Isaac, was born. God had kept His Word (like He always does) as the impossible had become possible.

Hebrews 11 tells us faith is having confidence what we hope for will actually happen; faith gives us assurance concerning things we don't yet see. It was by faith that Sarah was able to have a child, though she was barren and was too old. She had confidence that God would keep His promise. Today God has sons and daughters of promise He has ordained from before the foundation of the world. By faith, join the Spirit of God in calling them forth.

PRAYER

In the name of Jesus Christ, we call forth the Isaacs – God's children of promise. In the name of Jesus Christ, we curse unbelief and release faith to receive, so the plans of God are not aborted. In the name of Jesus Christ, we call forth those who will contend for the children of promise focusing on the One who promised, rather than present circumstances.

We declare all the promises of God are yes and amen in Christ Jesus (2 Cor. 1:20). We further declare neither delay of fulfillment nor disappointment will have any influence over conception or birth. We command wombs to open in Jesus' name receiving the life of God. We further declare, He is the giver of every good and perfect gift, and none of His purposes will be thwarted. In the name of Jesus Christ, we release God's high and holy purposes for each life birthed.

In the all-powerful name of Jesus Christ, amen.

A NEW IDENTITY

Jacob
Genesis 25-32

After Isaac and Rebekah had been married for twenty years, Rebekah became pregnant. The Lord told her the sons in her womb would become two rivaling nations, one nation would be stronger than the other, and the older son would serve the younger. (Gen. 25:23) It happened just as the Lord said. Esau, the firstborn, was Isaac's favorite; but Rebekah loved the younger son Jacob.

As the firstborn son, Esau was entitled to the birthright and the blessing; however, Esau sold his birthright to Jacob for bread and a pot of stew; thus, showing contempt for his rights as the firstborn. Sometime later Jacob deceived Isaac obtaining the blessing that was intended for Esau. From that time on, Esau hated Jacob and plotted how he would kill him after Isaac's death. In an effort to protect Jacob, Rebekah had Isaac send Jacob to her brother Laban's.

On his way to Laban's, Jacob found a good place to set up camp and stopped for the night. As he slept, he dreamed of a stairway reaching from earth up to heaven, and angels of God were going up and down the stairway. At the very top stood the Lord saying, "I am the Lord, the God of your grandfather Abraham, and the God of your father, Isaac," and God blessed him. (Gen. 28:11-15)

When Jacob awoke from his sleep, he said, "Surely the Lord is in this place, and I wasn't even aware of it." (vs. 16) But he was also afraid and said, "What an awesome place this is! It is none other than the house of God, the very gateway to heaven!" (vs. 17)

For 20 years, Jacob worked for Laban becoming very wealthy with a large family. Then the Lord told him to return to the land of his father assuring Jacob He would be with him.

Remembering how Esau wanted to kill him, Jacob sent his servants on ahead with many gifts, hoping to appease him. That night Jacob had an encounter with an angel of the Lord, wrestling with him until the break of dawn. When the angel saw he was not going to win over Jacob, he touched his hip, wrenching it out of its socket saying, "Let me go, for the dawn is breaking!" Jacob replied, "I will not let you go unless you bless me." The angel told him, "Your name will no longer be Jacob, but from now on you will be called Israel (meaning *prince with God*), because you have fought with God and with men and have won." (Gen. 32:28) Jacob looked up and saw Esau coming, and the two of them made peace.

This generation is filled with those God wants to meet through encounter, revealing Himself and giving them a new identity as a son or daughter. He has blessing after blessing to bestow upon them as they pursue Him and contend for the more of God. Join the Spirit of God in calling forth His sons and daughters.

PRAYER

In the name of Jesus Christ, we call forth all those God is waiting to encounter, revealing Himself and giving a new identity as a son or daughter. In the name of Jesus Christ, we call forth sons and daughters from the north, the south, the east and the west.

In the name of Jesus Christ, we call forth sons and daughters who will contend for the faith and for the more of God. We declare you are blessed. You are blessed in your going out and in your coming in. The work of your hands is blessed, and you have no lack. Because you are faithful in little, you will be trusted with much. We declare you will be about your Father's business in bringing His Kingdom to earth.

In Jesus' name, we call forth the peacemakers to positions of influence so volatile situations will be defused, bringing peace to nations.

To the glory of God, the Father, we pray and give thanks. Amen.

DREAMERS AND VISIONARIES

Joseph
Genesis 37 and 39

Joseph was one of twelve sons born to Jacob, the oldest son of his father's favorite wife, Rachel. Jacob loved Joseph more than his other sons and gave him a beautiful robe. As you can imagine, the ten older brothers were jealous of Joseph and couldn't say a kind word to him.

As a teenager, Joseph had two dreams of greatness. Wisdom would have led him to keep the dreams to himself, but at this point, Joseph wasn't known for his wisdom. He told his brothers the first dream saying, "We were out in the field, tying up bundles of grain. Suddenly my bundle stood up, and your bundles all gathered around and bowed low before mine." (vs.7) Joseph told the second dream to his brothers as well as his father saying, "The sun, moon and eleven stars bowed low before me." (vs. 9) Jealousy turned to hatred because of his dreams and the way he talked about them.

Hatred gave birth to evil. His brothers sold Joseph into slavery. They took his coat, dipped it in goat's blood, and took it back to Jacob with the report that Joseph was dead. According to the circumstances, Joseph's dreams were over. However, God had a plan.

As a slave, Joseph was falsely accused of attempted rape, he was thrown into prison for a crime he didn't commit; but Joseph guarded his heart, and everything he was assigned to do, he did with excellence. Bitterness was not able to form a root in him, and he kept his hope in God. Eventually he was released from prison and was placed second in command over all of Egypt. You can read the account in its entirety in Genesis 40 and 41. Because of a famine in the land, Jacob sent his sons to Egypt in search of grain, and, yes, his brothers came and bowed down low before him. Eventually, both dreams were fulfilled. It is an amazing story of forgiveness, redemption and restoration.

There are two verses in Joseph's story that continue to speak to me over and over again. In Jacob's last words to his sons, he says of Joseph, "Joseph is a fruitful vine, a fruitful vine near a spring, whose branches climb over a wall." (Gen. 49:22 NIV) The other is what Joseph speaks to his brothers after Jacob's death when they fear retaliation from him for what they have done in the past. He says, "But as for you, you meant evil against me; but God meant it for good, in order to bring it about as it is this day, to save many people alive. Now therefore, do not be afraid; I will provide for you and your little ones." (Gen. 50:20-21a NKJV)

In this generation, there are those in whom God has planted dreams and visions. These dreams and visions will restore family lines to health and wholeness, and produce solutions to the world's problems; but they have hit a wall. The wall may be family dysfunction, hatred, and unforgiveness – making them prisoners of bitterness, discouragement and hopelessness. Join the Spirit of God in calling forth these leaders in purity, wisdom, courage, forgiveness, and restoration.

PRAYER

In the name of Jesus Christ, we call forth all the Josephs, the dreamers and those with visions for solutions to the world's problems. In Jesus' name, we release the Spirit of Rapha to bring healing, health and wholeness to deep wounds. In the name of Jesus Christ, we curse the root of bitterness and command it to die. In Jesus' name, we call forth forgivers – those who let go of the past. We declare you bless those who wrong you, bringing salvation and restoration.

We declare you are fruitful vines, fruitful vines near a spring whose branches climb over a wall. We further declare what the enemy meant for evil against you, God means for good in order to save many people alive. We further declare no weapon formed against you will prosper, and none of God's purposes for you will be thwarted. We call forth sons and daughters to your destiny.

To the glory of God, the Father, amen.

FROM SLAVERY TO FREEDOM

Moses

Exodus 2-3

Amram and Jochebed were Israelites from the tribe of Levi. They married and had a baby at a time when the Israelites were slaves in Egypt. In order to keep the Israelites from becoming too strong, Pharaoh ordered that all Hebrew baby boys be killed. Jochebed made a basket, waterproofed it, and placed the basket with the baby inside, among the reeds along the Nile River. The baby's sister Miriam, stood watch to see what would become of him.

Pharaoh's daughter discovered the basket when she came to the river to bathe. She opened it, saw the little boy was crying, and felt sorry for him. Miriam stepped forward and asked if she should get a Hebrew woman to nurse the baby. The princess consented, and Miriam went and got her mother. When the boy was older, Jochebed brought him to Pharaoh's daughter who adopted him as her own. She named him Moses, meaning *lifted out of the water*.

Many years passed, and the king of Egypt died; however, the Israelites were still slaves working under brutal slave masters. They cried out, and God heard their cries. By this time, Moses was married and had been living east of Egypt in Midian for 40 years. At 80 years of age, when tending sheep in the wilderness of Mt. Sinai, Moses had an encounter with the Lord through a bush that was on fire, but did not burn up. The Lord told Moses He was sending him to Pharaoh; He also told Moses he would lead God's people Israel out of Egypt. (Ex. 3:10) However, Moses was resistant and asked God to send someone else. God showed him signs of His power and assured him He would be with him. Moses obeyed and God used him to deliver the children of Israel out of Egypt. In this generation, there are many trapped in human trafficking, terrorism and persecution that God wants to use to lead others to Himself. Join the Spirit of the Living God in calling forth His deliverers.

PRAYER

In the name of Jesus Christ, we call forth deliverers to set free victims from human trafficking, terrorism and persecution. We thank you, Lord, you never forget the ones forgotten by others, and you hear every one of their cries for justice. In Jesus' name, we command prison doors to open and captives to be set free.

In Jesus' name, we call forth leaders out of human trafficking to a life of salvation, deliverance, freedom and restoration. In Jesus' name, we call forth members of Isis, al-Qaeda and other terrorist organizations to have Damascus Road experiences so, like Saul, you will be changed. With the same passion you once served evil, you will now serve the true and living God.

In the name of the All-powerful One, Jesus Christ, and to His glory, amen.

SERVANT LEADERS

Joshua

Exodus 33; Numbers 13; 27; Deuteronomy 34

When it came time for the children of Israel to possess the land of Canaan, which God had promised them, God chose Joshua to succeed Moses as leader. Joshua was born a slave in Egypt with the name Hoshea (meaning *salvation*), but Moses changed his name to Joshua (meaning *the Lord is Salvation*). From the time he was a youth, he served as a close assistant to Moses. He was permitted to accompany Moses part way up Mt. Sinai when he received The Ten Commandments from God. Joshua had a heart for God and a hunger for His Presence. Moses would leave the Tent of Meeting after speaking with God, but Joshua would stay behind in the Tent of Meeting. (Ex. 33:11)

He also had a warrior's heart. When Amalek came to fight with Israel in Rephidim, Moses told Joshua to choose some men and go fight Amalek. Joshua was fearless, as he knew his help came from the Lord. He also knew Moses was on the hill with the Rod of God in his hand.

Joshua was one of the twelve men sent by Moses to explore the land of Canaan (Num. 13:16-17), and along with Caleb, they were the only ones who came back with an encouraging report. Jesus said the one who is greatest in the kingdom is the servant of all. He also said those who are faithful in little will receive much. Joshua, though a successful warrior, continued to be a servant to Moses. He was faithful.

So the Lord told Moses to lay his hands on Joshua and commission him to lead the people. He also told Moses to transfer some of his authority to him so the whole community of Israel would obey him. (Num. 27:18-20) Joshua was full of the spirit of wisdom and the people of Israel obeyed him.

In this generation, there are children who are hungry. They are hungry for God and hungry for His Presence. They long to minister to the Lord and serve Him by assisting leaders. However, many times they are overlooked because of their youth. Join the Spirit of God in calling forth these future leaders as well as those who will mentor them.

PRAYER

In the name of Jesus Christ, we call forth the Joshuas— leaders in the making who are willing to humble themselves in submission to serve and to be mentored by those who have come face to face with God. We call forth leaders who are bold, courageous and obedient, making it a priority to seek first the Kingdom of God and His righteousness. We call forth servant leaders who are themselves hungry to tarry with the Lord, soak in His Presence and come away with a readiness to, and expectation of, bringing Heaven down to earth impacting the nations.

In the name of Jesus Christ, we call forth mentors who, in turn, will call forth the gold in this generation, not looking down upon them because of their youth, but preparing them for spiritual battle, preparing them to host His Presence well and to lead nations into His inheritance. Thank you, Lord, for these servant leaders upon whom your Spirit rests. Amen.

STRONG IN THE LORD

Samson
Judges 13-16

Israel again did evil in the sight of the Lord; so, He allowed the Philistines to oppress them for 40 years. (Jud. 13:1). Among the Israelites there was a man from the tribe of Dan named Manoah. One day the angel of the Lord appeared to his wife and told her she would soon become pregnant and give birth to a son. (Before this, she had not been able to become pregnant.) He told her not to drink wine or any other alcoholic drink, nor to eat any forbidden food. He also told her the baby's hair must never be cut. He would be dedicated to God as a Nazirite from birth, and he would rescue Israel from the Philistines. The woman ran and told her husband about the angel and all he said.

Manoah prayed to the Lord asking for the angel to come back and give them more instructions about the son who was to be born. God answered Manoah's prayer, and the angel of God reappeared to his wife. She quickly went and got her husband, and the angel repeated the Lord's instructions.

Manoah invited the angel to stay and eat a meal with them. While the angel agreed to stay, he said he would not eat anything. He told Manoah he could prepare a burnt offering as a sacrifice to the Lord. So, Manoah took a young goat and a grain offering and offered it as a sacrifice to the Lord. As Manoah and his wife watched, the flames from the altar shot up toward the sky and the angel of the Lord ascended in the fire. When Manoah and his wife saw this, they fell with their faces to the ground. The angel did not reappear to Manoah or his wife, and Manoah finally realized it had been the angel of the Lord.

When the baby was born, his mother named him Samson. The Lord blessed him as he grew up, and the Spirit of the Lord began to move upon him. One time a young lion suddenly attacked Samson. The Spirit of the Lord came powerfully upon him, and he ripped the lion's jaws apart easily using only his bare hands.

But Samson had a weakness – Philistine women. He fell in love with a woman named Delilah. The rulers of the Philistines offered her 1,100 pieces of silver if she would find out from Samson the secret of his strength so they could capture him. Three different times she asked him the secret of his strength. Each time he lied to her. At any time, Samson could have walked away, but he did not. Finally, Samson got tired of the constant pestering, and he told her the truth revealing that his hair had never been cut, because He was dedicated to God as a Nazirite from birth. He confided in her that if his head were shaved, his strength would leave, and he would become as weak as anyone else. (Jud. 16:17) Delilah lulled him to sleep with his head in her lap, and then she called in a man to shave off his hair. Then she cried out as she had previously, "Samson! The Philistines have come to capture you!" (vs. 20) When he woke up, he thought he would shake free as before. Then the Bible states what, to me, is one of the saddest statements in Scripture: "But he didn't realize the Lord had left him." (vs. 20)

Samson was captured easily. They gouged out his eyes, bound him with chains and forced him to grind grain in the prison, but his hair began to grow back. During a great festival where the Philistines offered sacrifices and praised their god, Dagon, they brought Samson out to make sport of him.

Samson asked the young servant who was leading him by the hand to place his hands against the pillars that held up the temple. Samson prayed to the Lord asking him to please give him strength one more time. Then Samson pushed against the pillars asking the Lord to let him die with the Philistines, (vs. 30) and the temple crashed down on the Philistine rulers and the people. His brothers and other relatives went, got his body and buried him where his father Manoah was buried.

In this generation, there are young men and women the Lord wants to trust with great spiritual strength. Join the Spirit of God in calling them forth and praying prayers of protection over them.

PRAYER

In the name of Jesus Christ, we call forth young leaders who are strong in the Lord and in the power of His might. In the name of Jesus Christ, we declare you will make righteous choices and be protected from moral failure. We declare no weapon formed against you will prosper, and none of God's purposes for you will be thwarted. We further declare through your lives, you will be found faithful, not wavering, and you will finish strong, hearing the Lord say, "Well done."

In the name of Jesus Christ, we pray for those young leaders who have already been led astray. We pray they will once again hear the Spirit of the Lord, be reminded of God's goodness and come to repentance so they are restored, and once again strong in the Lord. Thank you, Lord, for your mercy and that you are the God who restores. In the merciful name of Christ Jesus, amen.

PROPHETS, PRIESTS AND JUDGES

Samuel
1 Samuel 1 and 3

At a time in Israel's history when "messages from the Lord were very rare, and visions were quite uncommon," (1 Sam. 3:1) there lived a couple from the tribe of Levi, Elkanah and his wife Hannah. Hannah was barren and grieved that she had no children.

In celebration of Passover each year, they would travel to Shiloh to worship the Lord. On one such trip, Hannah went to the Tabernacle to pray for a son. Out of desperation and anguish, Hannah cried bitterly and promised the Lord if He answered her prayer for a son, she would give him back to the Lord for his entire lifetime. As she left the Tabernacle, Eli, the priest, told her to go in peace saying, "May the God of Israel grant the request you have asked of him." (vs. 17) Hannah thanked him, and left to join the others, no longer sad.

In due time, Hannah gave birth to a son and named him Samuel meaning *asked of God*. When Samuel was weaned, Hannah kept her promise to the Lord. She took him to the Tabernacle in Shiloh, and they brought the boy to Eli saying the Lord had granted her request of several years earlier for a son and she was giving him to the Lord as she had promised.

Though Samuel was only a boy, he served the Lord by assisting Eli. He wore a linen garment like that of a priest. Each year his mother made a small coat for him and brought it to him when she came with her husband for the sacrifice. The Lord blessed Hannah and she gave birth to three sons and two daughters. Meanwhile, Samuel grew up in the Presence of the Lord.

One night as Samuel was sleeping in the Tabernacle near the Ark of God, suddenly the Lord called out, "Samuel." Thinking it was Eli calling him, Samuel got up, ran to Eli and said, "Here I am. Did you call me?" Eli answered he didn't call him, and told him to go back to bed. Then it happened a second time. Again, Eli told Samuel to go back to bed. Then the Lord called a third time; once again Samuel ran to Eli.

Finally Eli realized it was the Lord who was calling the boy and told him if he heard the call again, to say, "Speak, Lord, your servant is listening." Samuel went back to bed, and the Lord came and called as before. Samuel replied, "Speak, your servant is listening." Then the Lord spoke to Samuel.

The Bible says that the Lord was with Samuel, and everything he did proved to be reliable. Because of that, all Israel knew that Samuel was confirmed as a prophet of the Lord. The Lord continued to give messages to Samuel at the Tabernacle. Samuel's words then went out to all the people of Israel. Samuel served faithfully as prophet, priest and judge of Israel. He gave wise counsel, spoke the truth of God without compromise, and righteously judged Israel for the remainder of his life.

God is looking for those in this generation who will abide in His Presence with their ears tuned to hear His voice. He is looking for a generation who, upon hearing His voice, will speak the truth in love, reconciling the world to Himself through the Gospel of Jesus Christ. He is looking for a generation of judges who will make righteous judgments without any form of guile or corruption. He is also looking for a generation of intercessors who will be desperate for a move of God in this generation, who will cry out to God until they know that they have received the answer. Join with the Spirit of God in calling them forth.

PRAYER

In the name of Jesus Christ, we call forth prophets with the Spirit of Samuel who abide in the Lord's Presence and hear God's voice. We declare you are quick to obey, speaking the truth in love, reconciling the world to God through the Gospel of Jesus Christ.

In the name of Jesus Christ, we call forth priests who will minister before the Lord with pure hearts, clean hands and a mind that is set apart for His purposes.

In the name of Jesus Christ, we call forth judges who will make righteous judgments without guile or any form of corruption, always keeping in mind mercy triumphs over judgment.

In the name of Jesus Christ, we call forth intercessors with the Spirit of Hannah, who cry out to God, out of devotion to the Lord and out of desperation, for His prophets, priests and judges to be birthed in this generation. Amen.

SHEPHERD-KING

David
1 Samuel 16:1-13

When Saul was king of Israel, there was a young boy (probably 10-13 years of age) tending his father's sheep outside of Bethlehem – a job usually reserved for the least esteemed of the family or for its servants. While he may have been regarded by his family as the "least" solely because he was the youngest son, God in heaven did not look down upon him because of his youth. Rather, He saw a king!

So, God told Samuel to go to Bethlehem and find a man by the name of Jesse because He had chosen one of his sons to be Israel's next king. As Jesse's oldest son stood before Samuel, Samuel saw his appearance and height and thought surely he was the one the Lord had chosen. However, he was not. The Lord told Samuel not to make judgments based on appearance, because God looks at the heart. As Jesse's six other sons appeared before Samuel, the Lord told him they were not the one He had chosen.

Then Samuel learned of a younger son who was tending sheep in the field; so, he told Jesse to have him brought to him right away. When Samuel saw David, the Lord told him he was the one. So, Samuel anointed him with oil, and from that day on, the Spirit of the Lord was powerfully upon David.

When children come to Christ, they do not receive a junior-size Holy Spirit. The same Holy Spirit who raised Jesus from the dead resides in them. In fact, Jesus admonished us to be like little children when He said that unless we become like them we will never get into the Kingdom of Heaven. (Matt. 18:3) One of the most powerful prophetic words I ever received came through three young children. The Lord showed me what it was like to intercede with passion and with His heartbeat when I heard an elementary school boy lead his Sunday school class in prayer. It was a 5-year old girl during a soaking time at church who taught me how to climb up in Papa's lap to receive His love. Join the Spirit of God in calling forth the children of this generation, the beloved of the Father, who will chase after His own heart.

PRAYER

In the name of Jesus Christ, we say to the children of this generation who, like David, will chase after God's own heart, "Come forth!" We call forth children, filled with the Holy Spirit, anointed by God, who will reign in His Kingdom as sons and daughters. We declare children are treasures of the Kingdom and will not be overlooked or undervalued because of age, status or lack of education. We further declare out of your intimacy with Papa God the supernatural will flow, destroying the works of the devil.

We declare fathers and mothers, both physical and spiritual, will rise up to train this generation enabling them to reach their full, God-given potential. We declare you will bless, encourage, strengthen, empower, and release this generation to do the works of Jesus to the glory of God, the Father. In His holy name, amen.

DAY 9

ANOINTED WORSHIP LEADERS

David
1 Samuel 16:14-23

In 1 Samuel 15 we read the Lord was sorry He ever made Saul king because of his disloyalty and refusal to obey the Lord's command. So, the Spirit of the Lord left Saul and a tormenting spirit filled him with depression and fear.

In Hebrew, the word *zamar* means to touch the strings or to pluck the strings and sing along in praise to God. This type of praise can shift atmospheres. Such was the music that David played. So, David was brought in to serve in Saul's court. Whenever the tormenting spirit troubled Saul, David would play the lyre or harp. Then Saul would feel better and the tormenting spirit would go away.

God is raising up a new generation of worship leaders who will lead others into the Presence of God and whose music will shift atmospheres bringing God's Kingdom to earth. Join the Holy Spirit in calling forth these young anointed worship leaders.

PRAYER

In the name of Jesus Christ, we call forth worship leaders with the heart of David who are anointed to lead others into God's Presence, drawing them into the very heart of God. We declare as you host the Presence, you will take anointed worship to houses of worship, streets, marketplaces, places of entertainment, houses of education, halls of government, and trading floors of economics.

We declare when you play upon your instruments, new songs will come forth and entire atmospheres will shift, bringing God's order out of chaos. We further declare when the sounds of Heaven come forth through your instruments and song, extraordinary miracles will burst forth bringing God's Kingdom here to earth. To the glory of God, the Father, amen.

YOUNG WARRIORS

David
1 Samuel 17:1-51

When David was a teenager (probably 15-17 years old), the Philistines gathered their army for battle against the Israelites. Saul countered by gathering his Israelite troops; and the two armies faced each other from opposite hills, with a valley between them.

Goliath, a Philistine champion who was over nine feet tall, came out and shouted a taunt across to the Israelites, saying, "Choose one man to come down here and fight me! If he kills me, then we will be your slaves. But if I kill him, you will be our slaves! I defy the armies of Israel today! Send me a man who will fight me!" (vs. 8-10) When Saul and the Israelites heard this, they were terrified and deeply shaken.

Jesse sent David to check on his brothers who were part of Saul's army as well as to take them food. When David heard and saw what was happening, he asked, "Why is that pagan Philistine allowed to defy the armies of the living God?" David's question was reported to Saul, and the king sent for him. David volunteered to fight Goliath, but Saul told him there was no way he could fight and win because he was only a boy. The Philistine had been a man of war since his youth.

However, David persisted, recounting how in taking care of his father's flock, he rescued lambs out of the mouths of bears and lions, clubbing them to death. He declared, "The Lord who rescued me from the lion and the bear will rescue me from this Philistine." Finally Saul consented to allow David to fight and offered him his armor to wear in the battle. However, David wasn't used to wearing armor; so, he wore his normal clothing.

Then David went to a stream, picked up five smooth stones (Goliath had 4 brothers) and put them in his shepherd's bag. As Goliath taunted, David replied, "You come to me with sword, spear, and javelin, but I come to you in the name of the Lord of Heaven's Armies;" (vs. 45) and David triumphed over the Philistine with only a sling and a stone. God has in this generation young warriors who will go to the river of God in worship and intercession, gathering the weapons to defeat the enemy and plunder his camp in the power of the Holy Spirit. Join the Spirit of God in calling them forth.

PRAYER

In the name of Jesus Christ, we call out to the young warriors who will not shrink back in fear, "Arise!" Come to the river of God and gather your weapons of intercession, thanksgiving, praise, dance and worship.

We declare you will defeat giants through the power of the Holy Spirit. We further declare out of a heart of intimacy and worship, you will plunder the camp of the enemy; taking back everything stolen, so the whole world will know the Lord, He is God! Thank you, Triumphant Lord, for the victory! Amen.

DEATH TO LIFE

Widow's Son
1 Kings 17:8-24

During a severe draught in Israel, the Lord told the prophet Elijah to go to the village of Zarephath, where he would find a widow who would give him food to eat. As he arrived at the village gate, he saw a widow gathering sticks and asked her for a drink of water as well as a piece of bread. She replied that she had no bread in the house, only a little flour and oil that she was going to cook for her and her son. It was going to be their last meal before they died of starvation.

Through her obedience to the Lord's word through Elijah, the widow, her son and Elijah continued to eat for many days. There was always enough flour and oil left in the containers, just as the Lord had promised through Elijah.

Sometime later, the woman's son became sick and died. Elijah took the child's body from her arms and carried him up the stairs to the room where he had been staying. After laying the child on the bed, Elijah stretched himself out over the boy three times and cried out to the Lord for the child's life to return. The third time he did this the boy revived. He was alive! Elijah took the boy back to his mother, and she knew for sure Elijah was a man of God through whom the Lord spoke.

In 33 A.D., there was another Son of a widow who had died and been buried, but on the third day, the Spirit of God raised Him from the dead, and death was defeated forevermore. Join the Spirit of God in calling to life – a life of destiny and purpose – the children in this generation who are dead in trespasses and sin.

PRAYER

In the name of Jesus Christ, we say to those dead in trespasses and sin, "Come forth!" We declare you are a new creation in Christ Jesus. The old life is gone; everything is now brand new. You are no longer a slave to sin or fear; you are now a child of God. In the name of Jesus Christ, we curse addictions to drugs, sex and alcohol, and we declare they no longer have any hold over you. You have been set free.

We declare God is good, and He has good plans for your life. We further declare no weapon formed against you will prosper, and none of God's plans for you will be thwarted, for you are the beloved of the Father. In His precious name, amen.

EMPTY VESSELS FILLED TO ABUNDANCE

Widow and Two Sons

2 Kings 4:1-7

One day the widow of a student who was a prophet under Elisha came to him asking for help. A creditor was threatening to take her two sons as slaves because she couldn't pay her debt. Elisha asked her what she had in her house, and she told him she had nothing except a flask of oil. He instructed her to borrow as many empty jars as she could from her neighbors. Then she was to go into her house with her sons, pour the oil out that was in the flask filling one container at a time until they were all full. She did as Elisha told her, and soon every container was full to the brim! Then she was able to sell the oil, pay her debts, and she and her sons lived on what was left over.

In this generation, there are children of God who have large amounts of student loans and credit card debt, are living under a poverty mindset, and are captives of fear. Join the Spirit of God in declaring His provision of abundance and freedom.

Note that it was the woman who determined how much oil she received. I believe that if she had borrowed more containers, she would have received more. God is looking for those in this generation who will not be content with what they have spiritually, but will with hunger, thanksgiving and intimacy press into the more of God.

PRAYER

In the name of Jesus Christ, we call forth those who suffer lack to receive abundance from the unlimited resources of the Father. We cast down the orphan spirit as well as the spirit of poverty and command them to be gone in Jesus' name. We release the Spirit of adoption to sons and daughters, and release the Spirit of abundance to replace the spirit of poverty. We declare the Word of God that He provides above and beyond what we can ask or think. (Eph. 3:20) We further declare, "No good thing will He withhold from those who walk uprightly" (Ps. 84:11 NKJV), and "I was young and now I am old. Yet I have never seen the godly abandoned or their children begging for bread." (Ps. 37:25)

We further declare, "God has not given [you] a spirit of fear, but of power and of love and of a sound mind." (2 Tim. 1:7 NKJV)

In the name of Jesus Christ, we call forth sons and daughters to bring your empty vessels (yourselves) to Jesus to be filled with the oil of the Holy Spirit and power. We declare you have a hunger and thirst for the Presence that can only be satisfied temporarily, and out of a heart of thanksgiving and intimacy, you will continually press in for the more of God. To Him who is calling you, be glory, amen.

SERVANT EVANGELISTS

Naaman's Maid
2 Kings 5:1-19

Naaman was the chief military commander of the Syrian army. The King of Syria had great admiration for Naaman because the Lord had given him great victories and he was a mighty warrior. While Naaman was a powerful military leader, he was sick. He had a terrible skin disease called leprosy. Today there is a cure for leprosy, but in Naaman's time, there was no medical cure. So, the prognosis for Naaman was a long, painful death.

Living in Naaman's home was a young Israeli girl who had been taken captive during one of Syria's raids in Israel. She served in Naaman's home as his wife's maid. She could have been fearful or bitter over having been taken away from her family and from her own home. However, instead, she was filled with compassion. One day she told her mistress she wished her master would go see the prophet Elisha in Samaria so he could be healed of his leprosy.

Naaman told the king of Aram what she had said, and the king wrote letters of introduction for Naaman to give to the King of Israel. You can imagine the reaction of the king of Israel. He tore his clothes in dismay saying, "Am I God, that

I can give life and take it away?" (vs. 7) When Elisha heard about it, he sent a message to the king of Israel telling him to send Naaman to him.

Upon arrival at his house, Elisha sent a messenger out telling Naaman to go wash himself seven times in the Jordan River. Then he would be healed. Naaman was insulted! First of all, Elisha didn't give him the honor that he was used to receiving. Second, the Jordan River would have been muddy, and he didn't want to get in it. Many times we miss God because He does not do things the way we think He will. Naaman almost missed the healing God had for him because he didn't want to humble himself and obey.

Naaman's officers tried to reason with him and encouraged him to do as he had been instructed. So, Naaman went down to the Jordan River and dipped himself seven times. When he came up out of the water the seventh time, his skin became as healthy as that of a young child. He was completely healed! Then Naaman and his entire party went back to find Elisha, and Naaman declared there was no God in the entire world except in Israel.

This miracle took place because of the compassion and courage of a young servant girl. God is looking for those in this generation who are willing to go low in humility to serve others, and in the Spirit of love and compassion share the good news of Jesus Christ. Join the Spirit of God in calling them forth.

PRAYER

In the name of Jesus Christ, we call forth servant evangelists – those with a spirit of compassion who are willing to go low in humility to serve others. We release these servant evangelists to homes, marketplaces and places of education who will boldly declare and demonstrate the good news of salvation, healing and deliverance.

In the name of Jesus Christ, we cast down all judgmentalness, blame and shame; and in the name of Jesus Christ, we release the spirit of forgiveness to be expressed in love through words and works of the Kingdom of Heaven. Even so, Lord, let it be. Amen.

RIGHTEOUS YOUNG LEADERS

King Josiah
2 Kings 22-23:25

Amon was twenty-two years old when he became king of Judah, but he reigned in Jerusalem for only two years. The Bible tells us that he did evil in the Lord's sight worshipping man-made idols just as his father had done. He abandoned the Lord God, and he refused to follow the Lord's ways. His own officials conspired against him and assassinated him in his palace.

It is out of this family history that Josiah is born. Josiah was eight years old when his father was assassinated, and he became king of Judah in his place. He reigned in Jerusalem for 31 years, and the hallmark of his reign is found in 2 Kings 22:2 which says, "He did what was pleasing in the Lord's sight and followed the example of his ancestor David. He did not turn away from doing what was right."

When Josiah was twenty-six years old, he gave instructions for the Lord's Temple to be cleaned, repaired and restored. It was during the cleaning of the temple that a scroll, the Book of the Law, was found. It was brought to King Josiah, and he had the court secretary read it to him. When he heard the Word of the Lord, he tore his clothes in despair, for Josiah and the people had not been worshipping God or obeying His Word. Josiah instituted several religious reforms to lead the people back to the Lord God, to worship Him alone.

There had not been a Passover celebration since the time when the judges ruled in Israel, nor throughout all the years of the kings of Israel and Judah; but in the eighteenth year of King Josiah's reign, the Passover was celebrated. God wants to redeem nations and generations through young men and women like King Josiah, who will reign as sons and daughters of the King of Kings. Join the Spirit of God in calling them forth.

PRAYER

In the name of Jesus Christ, we call forth today's Josiahs, young leaders, who will hunger and thirst for God's Word, His Kingdom and His righteousness. We declare the Word of God, "Christ has redeemed you from the curse of the Law" (Gal. 3:13 NKJV) so the sins of past generations will not be found in you.

We declare you have ears to hear what the Lord is saying and a heart that is quick to obey His Voice. We declare you will lead by example in love and purity so that nations are changed in a day, seeking God alone and following after Him with a whole heart.

Amen.

VOICES OF COMPASSION

Jeremiah
Jeremiah 1:4-10

In the thirteenth year of King Josiah's reign, the Lord gave Jeremiah this message, "I knew you before I formed you in your mother's womb. Before you were born I set you apart and appointed you as my prophet to the nations." (vs. 5) When Jeremiah heard the Lord's message, he protested saying he was too young. The Lord assured Jeremiah he was not too young; He told him not to fear, for He had put His words in his mouth.

Jeremiah did speak for God. He showed great compassion for his people and wept over them. He suffered much at their hands, but he forgave them. As such, Jeremiah is perhaps one of the most Christ-like personalities in the Old Testament.

Jeremiah, like the other prophets in the Old Testament, was under the Old Covenant. As such, he was a mouthpiece for God - speaking God's words of instruction, warning, prophecy and judgment upon people and nations who were living in disobedience to God.

However, prophecy under the New Covenant is for strengthening, encouragement, and comfort. (1 Cor. 14:3) Every believer can speak such prophecy. Those holding the office of the prophet today, along with apostles, evangelists, pastors and teachers, equip God's people so they can be healthy - growing in maturity and full of love. (Eph. 4:11-16)

Join the Spirit of God in calling forth the prophetic voices of today. Join those who will speak the truth in love bringing strength, encouragement and comfort to the body of Christ; who through the compassion of Christ will call forth the gold in the sons and daughters who don't yet know Him.

PRAYER

In the name of Jesus Christ, we call forth the prophetic voices of today, those who will listen carefully for God's voice, wait to hear what He says, and then speak His message of love, affirmation and empowerment. We call forth those who will speak words of strength, comfort, and encouragement to the body of Christ so she becomes a body that is healthy, growing in maturity and filled with love.

We call forth prophets who will speak His truth in love causing nations as well as individuals to turn back to loving the Lord God, so hearts are restored to the Father, so all people taste His joy and goodness resulting in God's love being poured out even more on His children.

Thank you, Lord, for those who listen to You, then speak. Amen.

LIVING IN WHOLENESS

Daniel and Friends
Daniel 1

During the reign of King Jehoiakim of Judah, King Nebuchadnezzar of Babylon came to Jerusalem and besieged it taking sacred objects from the Temple of God as well as taking captives. The king ordered his chief of staff to bring to the palace some of the young men of Judah's royal family and other noble families - those who were well versed in every branch of learning, gifted with knowledge and good judgment, and suited to serve in the royal place. They would be trained in the local language and literature, and after three years of training, they would enter the royal service. Among the captives selected were four strong, healthy, good-looking young men named Daniel, Hananiah, Mishael and Azariah. Daniel's friends are best known for their Babylonian names: Shadrach, Meshach and Abednego.

The king assigned them a daily ration of food and wine from his own kitchens, "but Daniel was determined not to defile himself by eating the food and wine given to them by the king." (vs. 8) Instead, he asked the attendant assigned to them, to serve them a diet of vegetables and water for a test period of ten days. At the end of the ten-day test, Daniel and his three friends looked healthier and better nourished than the young men who had been eating the food assigned by the king. In addition, God gave them unusual aptitude for understanding. God gave Daniel the special ability to interpret the meanings of dreams and visions.

Jesus taught it is not what goes into a person that defiles that person, but rather the words that come out of him/her (from the heart). (Matt. 15:11) As temples of the Holy Spirit (1 Cor. 6:19), the Lord wants His children healthy in spirit, soul and body. (3 John 2) However, there is an enemy who comes to steal, kill and destroy. (John 10:10) Feeding on the Word of God, spending time in His Presence and having an attitude of thankfulness will help eliminate worry, fear, stress, and depression, which the enemy can use to rob us of the joy and peace God intends for us. Making good choices for your body in diet, exercise and rest are crucial for a healthy lifestyle.

Just as in Daniel's day, God is looking in this generation to pour out blessings of health and wholeness on those who will yield their bodies to Him as living sacrifices. Join the Spirit of God in calling them forth.

PRAYER

In the name of Jesus Christ, we call out to the body of Christ, "Come forth; be healed and walk in wholeness." We declare God's Word "that you may prosper in all things and be in health, just as your soul prospers." (3 John 2 NKJV) We further declare you are redeemed from the curse of the law. (Gal. 3:13 NKJV)

You are blessed. You are holy and without blame before Him and free from condemnation. You are His elect, chosen by Him and more than a conqueror. You are accepted in the Beloved, and you are gifted by Him to live a revival lifestyle to His glory. Amen.

FAITHFUL IN PERSECUTION

Shadrach, Meshach and Abednego
Daniel 3:1-30

King Nebuchadnezzar made a gold statue ninety feet tall and nine feet wide and held a special dedication when the statue was set in place. During the dedication a herald shouted the king's command; when the horn, flute, zither, lyre, harp, pipes, and other musical instruments were heard, the people were to bow to the ground in worship of the statue. Anyone who refused to obey the king's command would immediately be thrown into a blazing furnace.

So, at the sound of the musical instruments, all the people, regardless of their race or language, bowed to the ground and worshipped the statue – all except Shadrach, Meshach and Abednego. Their refusal to bow down and worship the statue was reported to the king. Nebuchadnezzar flew into a rage; he was so angry his face became distorted with rage. He had the three young men brought to him and gave them another chance to obey his command.

They did not bow down saying, "If we are thrown into the blazing furnace, the God whom we serve is able to save us. He will rescue us from your power, Your Majesty. But even if he doesn't ... we will never serve your gods or worship the gold statue you have set up." (vs. 17-18) The king was so angry that he ordered the furnace be heated seven times hotter than usual. The three young men were bound and thrown in the furnace; however, because the fire was so hot, the flames killed the soldiers as they threw the three young men in.

Suddenly, Nebuchadnezzar shouted, "I see four men, unbound, walking around in the fire unharmed! And the fourth looks like a god." (vs. 25) He shouted for Shadrach, Meshach, and Abednego to come out. When they stepped out of the furnace, the crowd, which had gathered, saw the fire had not touched them. Not a hair on their heads was singed, their clothing was not scorched; in fact, they didn't even smell of smoke!

Nebuchadnezzar gave praise to the Lord God for saving them. Then he made a decree no one was to speak a word against the God of Shadrach, Meshach and Abednego, or they would be torn from limb to limb. Afterwards, he promoted the three young men to even higher positions in the province of Babylon.

God is looking for a generation strong in the Lord and in the power of His might - a generation who will not bend the knee even in the face of persecution, but rather, will remain loyal to their God. Join the Spirit of God in calling them forth.

PRAYER

In the name of Jesus Christ, we call forth the Shadrachs, Meshachs and Abednegos of today, those who will not compromise their loyalty to the Lord God when being pressured. We declare you are strong in the Lord and in the power of His might, and you will bow down to no other than the true and living God even under threat of persecution.

We bless with the Presence of God all those enduring persecution in places of great darkness so all fear has to flee. In the name of Jesus Christ, we release the Spirit of Shalom over you; even as you face a blazing furnace or any other means of death, you will have perfect peace. We declare by your faithfulness and the One present in you, upon you, and around you, evil captors will lay their weapons down and declare, "There is no other god who can rescue like this! The Lord He is God. There is no other beside Him." Amen.

DAY 18

ANOINTED WITH WISDOM AND POWER

Boy Jesus
Luke 2:41-52

While growing up, Jesus lived in the town of Nazareth with his parents, Mary and Joseph. From Nazareth to Jerusalem was about a five-day walk, if the roads were dry and they weren't clogged up with travelers. Jesus' parents traveled this road every year as they made their way to Jerusalem to celebrate the Passover festival. When Jesus was twelve years old, the family made the annual trip to Jerusalem as usual.

After the celebration was over, they started their journey back to Nazareth. Jesus wasn't with them, but at first, they didn't notice He was missing. Being a twelve-year-old boy, they assumed He was with relatives or friends. However, when He didn't show up that evening, they began to search for Him among the other travelers. Jesus was nowhere to be found. So, Mary and Joseph headed back to Jerusalem. They searched for Him for two days, and on the third day, they found Him in the Temple with religious leaders, listening to them talk and asking them questions. Those who heard Him were amazed at His answers and His understanding.

His parents didn't know what to think. His mother asked why He had done this to them, they had been frantically

57

searching for Him everywhere. He replied, "But why did you need to search? Didn't you know that I must be in my Father's house." (Luke 2:49) They didn't understand what He meant. Jesus returned home with Mary and Joseph and was obedient to them. He continued to grow in stature, in wisdom and in favor with God and all the people.

The Lord is looking for youngsters in this generation, who have a hunger for God and for His Word in whom He can plant wisdom beyond their years as well as understanding and favor. Join the Spirit of God in calling them forth.

PRAYER

In the name of Jesus Christ, we say to those in this generation who have a hunger for God and His Word, "Come forth!" In the name of Jesus Christ, we release in you the Spirit of wisdom and might.

We declare you will confound leaders of religion, not by persuasive argument, but by demonstrations of power through the love of God and His Spirit. We declare because of the Spirit upon you, you will have favor with God and man, and He will open doors to you so with His wisdom, you will influence governments, universities and nations bringing them under His divine authority. Amen.

TAKING JESUS AT HIS WORD

Nobleman's Son Healed
John 4:46-54

Jesus was in Cana of Galilee when a government official from nearby Capernaum made his way to Him. The official's son was sick, near death. When he heard Jesus was in the area, he came and asked Jesus to come and heal his son. Jesus didn't go with him; rather, he told the official, "Go back home. Your son will live." (vs. 50) The official believed what Jesus said and started home.

On his way home, his servants came and told him his son was alive and well. He asked when his son started to get better, and they told him his fever suddenly disappeared the afternoon before. The father realized it was the very same time Jesus said to him, "Your son will live." As a result of this miracle, the man and his whole household believed in Jesus.

The Lord is looking for those in this generation who will take Him at His Word and believe, putting feet to their faith. He is looking not only for those who know the Word, but, rather, for those who will live it and move out in its authority on behalf of others. Join the Spirit of God in calling them forth.

PRAYER

We declare, according to the Word of God, everyone who came to Jesus for healing was made well. We further declare 1 Peter 2:24, "by His wounds you have been healed." In the name of Jesus Christ, we call to this generation, "Believe and receive."

We further declare you know Him and His Word, which is alive in you. Because you believe and take Him at His Word, we declare like those who have gone before you, you will overthrow kingdoms, rule with justice and receive what God has promised you. You will declare the goodness of God by your words and by His works in you so you see others come to Him in repentance receiving salvation, healing and deliverance – all for His glory. Amen.

DEATH TO LIFE

Widow's Son from Nain
Luke 7:11-17

Jesus and His disciples were walking to the village of Nain with a large crowd following Him. As He approached the gate, a funeral procession was coming out of the village. The funeral was for a boy – the only son of a widow. As you can imagine, a large crowd from the village was with her.

When Jesus saw her, His heart overflowed with compassion, and He told her not to cry. He went over to the coffin and touched it. Then He commanded the young man to get up. (vs. 14) The young boy sat up and began to talk! Then Jesus gave the boy back to his mother. When the people saw it, they were filled with awe and praised God!

While Jesus was doing something ordinary – walking to a village, He made room for the extraordinary to happen. While He was surrounded by people, He saw the one who was in front of Him, and He stopped for that one. Love always sees the one. Love always takes time for the one. Jesus came to destroy the works of the devil (1 John 3:8) and to give abundant life (John 10:10). In this case, He did both. He defeated death, and gave life both to the boy as well as to his mother. I am sure, when she held her son again, her life revived and joy was restored.

God is looking for those in this generation who will carry His Presence and be willing to stop for the one He places in front of them, bringing them life, health, hope and soundness. Join the Spirit of God in calling them forth.

PRAYER

In the name of Jesus Christ, we call forth the lovers of God who carry His Presence and are willing to stop for the one He places in front of you. We declare the Lord directs your steps, and He goes before you guiding your pathway. We further declare as you take risk, He will prepare the ones He places in front of you so they are willing to receive ministry.

We declare you will discover His treasures in the most unlikely places, you will set captives free, and they will leave your presence rejoicing because of what the Lord has done. We declare you are a history maker and a world changer because of the anointing upon you from the One who is in you. To Him be glory forever and ever. Amen.

HUMILITY AND FAITH

Jairus' Daughter Raised
Matthew 9:18-26; Mark 5:21-43; Luke 8:40-56

The people had been waiting for Jesus to cross the Sea of Galilee, and as soon as He came to shore, the crowds welcomed Him. Jairus, a leader from the synagogue, came and knelt before Jesus pleading for Him to come and heal his only daughter who was sick and dying. As Jesus began to go with Him, He was stopped by a woman who came through the crowd and touched the hem of His garment. The woman was instantly healed after having been sick for 12 years. While Jesus was speaking with her, a messenger from Jairus' home came saying his daughter had died. Jesus overheard the conversation and told Jairus not to fear, but believe.

When they got to Jairus' home, a crowd of professional mourners were weeping and wailing as they were paid to do. Jesus, knowing what He was about to do, told them the little girl wasn't dead, but sleeping. They laughed at Him in ridicule, and He told them to leave. Then, taking only Peter, James and John with Him, along with the girl's father and mother, Jesus went inside where the 12-year old girl lay. He took her by the hand and called in a loud voice, "My child, get up!" At that moment, her life returned, and her parents were filled with awe at what just happened. Jesus instructed them to give their daughter something to eat.

The Lord is looking for those like Jairus who will father this generation in humility and faith - through intercession, building relationships, and mentoring through demonstration and power of the Word modeled in their lives. Join the Spirit of God in calling them forth.

PRAYER

In the name of Jesus Christ, we call forth men of God to father this generation so by your authenticity they become lovers of God with their identity secure in the Beloved. We declare as you come along side and mentor them in pursuing the more of God, your ceiling will become their floor.

We further declare their hearts will be settled forever on the fact that God is good all the time. We declare out of intimacy with Christ, they will partner with Him in destroying the works of the devil and bringing His Kingdom to earth for His glory alone. Amen.

GIVING ALL

Boy with Loaves and Fish

Matthew 14:13-21; Mark 6:30-44; Luke 9:10-17; John 6:1-14

Everywhere Jesus went, the crowds followed Him. There were so many people coming and going that Jesus and His disciples didn't even have time to eat. On one occasion, Jesus suggested to His disciples they go and find a quiet place where they could rest for a while. However, when the people saw them get into a boat, they followed after them along the shore. When Jesus and the disciples got to the other side of the sea, the crowd had already gathered.

Instead of being upset or disappointed they didn't get rest, when Jesus saw the huge crowd gathered, He was moved with compassion toward the people saying they were like sheep without a shepherd. So, He began teaching them many things about the Kingdom of God. He also healed those who were sick.

Late in the afternoon, the disciples came to Jesus and asked Him to send the crowds away so they could buy food to eat. Jesus told the disciples to feed them. They looked to see what food was available, but only Andrew found food; a boy had five small barley loaves and two fish, which he willingly gave to Jesus. Jesus told the disciples to have the people

65

sit down on the grassy slopes in groups of 50 or 100. He took the bread, gave thanks to God and began breaking it off for the disciples to give out to the people. He did the same with the fish. All the people ate as much as they wanted, and so there would be no waste, Jesus had the disciples gather up the leftovers. There were 12 baskets full left over after 5,000 men in addition to women and children had eaten their fill.

This miracle happened because one boy gave Jesus all he had. Because of his generosity, he had the blessing of seeing his lunch feed all the people (as well as himself) – with an abundance left over! God is looking for His children in this generation who will seek first the Kingdom of God and His righteousness. He is looking for those who will give unselfishly and generously so He can multiply what is given to provide nourishment for others as well as a blessing that is pressed down, shaken together and running over for the person who gives. Join the Spirit of God in calling them forth.

PRAYER

In the name of Jesus Christ, we call forth children of God to seek first the Kingdom of Heaven and His righteousness giving your all to Him. We declare as you surrender your all to Him, He becomes Lord of your time, your resources, and your life.

We further declare as you spend time with Him, He will reveal to you secrets from His Word He has hidden just for you to find.

We further declare as you give generously and unselfishly, you will become a resource for Heaven so thousands will be nourished through what you give. We further declare because you give generously, you will receive a good measure, pressed down, shaken together and running over, poured into your lap (Lk. 6:38). We declare over you the righteous are never forsaken and their children are never begging for bread. All your needs are met in Christ Jesus, and you will always have enough to share with someone else.

We further declare because your life is poured out as an offering to Him, you will be standing firm like a flourishing tree planted by God's design, deeply rooted by the brooks of bliss; bearing fruit in every season of your life. You are never dry, never fainting, ever blessed, ever plentiful (Ps. 1:3 TPT). Amen.

THE POWER OF BEING AUTHENTIC
A Gentile Woman
Matthew 15:21-28; Mark 7:24-30

Frequently throughout the Gospels we see the Jews addressed Jesus as the Son of David. The title is used by those seeking healing, such as the two blind men (Matt. 9:27) as well as blind Bartimaeus. (Mk. 10:47), by the people (Matt. 10:23), as well as by the crowds who praised Him during His triumphal entry. (Matt. 21:9) However, in this instance, the title is spoken by a gentile Canaanite woman when approaching Jesus about healing her daughter from an evil spirit. Matthew says Jesus didn't say even a word to her. Could it be He didn't answer her because she was pretending to be something she was not? Perhaps she was coming to Him out of entitlement as a Jew rather than being authentic with Him. It is something to consider.

The mother kept begging for help, and the disciples urged Jesus to send her away. However, He did not. Suddenly, there is a shift in the woman's attitude. For the first time, she comes in worship, pleading again, "Lord, help me." (Matt. 15:25) It is then that Jesus responds to her. He tells her it is not right to feed the children's (Jew's) food to puppies (Gentiles), and the woman replies saying even puppies are allowed to eat the scraps that fall from the table. Jesus then calls her "dear woman," recognizes her great faith, and grants her request. Her daughter was instantly healed. (vs. 28) God is looking for a generation of worshippers who will come to Him in faith and humility, worshipping with hearts of transparency. Join the Spirit of God is calling forth these worshippers.

PRAYER

In the name of Jesus Christ, we call forth a generation of worshippers who will come to the Lord in faith and humility, worshipping with hearts of transparency. We declare your worship brings the Presence of God. We further declare, as you focus on Him, you will find all of your needs are met. In His Presence, there is peace. In His Presence, there is fullness of joy; so all depression must leave. In His Presence, there is freedom; all chains are broken. In His Presence, there is salvation, healing, and deliverance. No weapon of the enemy can survive His Presence. In His Presence, there is hope for the hopeless. In His Presence, there is JESUS! In His Presence, there is victory! In Jesus' name, we declare your worship brings Him. Hallelujah! Amen.

PEACE IN THE PLACE OF CHAOS

Boy Healed

Matthew 17:14-21; Mark 9:14-29; Luke 9:37-42

Jesus was on a high mountain with Peter, James and John when He suddenly transfigured before them. His face shone like the sun, and His clothes became white as snow. Moses and Elijah appeared and began talking to Him. What an amazing scene!

However, down at the bottom of the mountain something entirely different was taking place. In desperation, a father had brought his only son to the disciples for healing. His son had seizures and was unable to speak. The son was living in torment, a prisoner in his own body. When Jesus came down from the mountain, He learned the remaining disciples had not been able to help the boy. So, Jesus rebuked the demon; it came out of him, and the child was healed.

Later the disciples came to Jesus privately and asked why they were unable to cast out the demon. Jesus said it was because of their unbelief. In the gospel of Mark it says that particular demon does not go out except by prayer and fasting.

We are living in a time when it seems the number of children suffering from brain disorders is on the rise. ADD,

ADHD, epilepsy, autism, dementia and Down syndrome are surfacing at alarming rates, taking many children captive. Please do not misunderstand what I am saying. Children are a blessing from the Lord. (Ps. 127:3) Each and every child is a precious gift from God – period. The child is a wonderful gift; the disease or disorder is not. God is good. He gives good gifts to his children. (James 1:17) It is Satan who is the robber and the destroyer. (John 10:10) Jesus came to destroy the works of the devil. (1 John 3:8) He came to set captives free. He set the boy in the above passages free, and He wants to set children free today.

The Lord is looking for those who love Him, who will press into Him for the healing and deliverance of these children held hostage by the enemy. Join the Spirit of God in calling forth intercessors as well as those equipped in the power of the Holy Spirit to bring healing and deliverance to these precious children.

PRAYER

To all children held hostage by the enemy with brain injuries, diseases or disorders, we declare you are a perfect gift from God. We further declare no weapon formed against you will prosper and none of His purposes for you will be thwarted. In the name of Jesus Christ, we release the Shalom of Heaven to bring peace and order out of chaos. In the name of Jesus Christ, we declare healing and restoration over you right now.

To the parents, we declare you are blessed. Your marriage is blessed, and your family is blessed. We further declare you have wisdom from above to balance the needs of your special child with the needs of each other and those of your family. We declare the Lord gives you supernatural strength to walk in His love and live out of the well of His abundant joy.

In the name of Jesus Christ, we call forth sons and daughters who love God and will press into Him with worship, thanksgiving, praise and intercession on behalf of the children held hostage by the enemy. We declare your worship brings the Presence of God, and where the Presence is, there is health, wholeness and soundness.

We call forth a generation who are fearless because they walk in light of their identity as sons and daughters of God. We further declare the works of the devil do not intimidate them, because they know the One living in them is much greater. We declare when they see a child, they see the child through the eyes of Jesus; they are moved with the compassion of Jesus; they see a child totally whole; and in Jesus' name, they call wholeness forth, bringing His Kingdom to earth. In His all-powerful name, amen.

SONS AND DAUGHTERS CALLED HOME

The Prodigal Son

Luke 15:11-32

The Pharisees and teachers of religious law complained about Jesus associating with sinful people such as tax collectors and notorious sinners. In response, Jesus told them the following story. A certain man had two sons. The youngest son came to his father and demanded he be given his share of the inheritance before his father's death. A few days later, he packed up his belongings and left home. He went to a land far from home where he could spend his inheritance without his father's influence, criticism or oversight. He ended up wasting all the money he had on wild living.

About the same time he ran out of money, a famine swept through the land, and the son began to be in want. He got a job feeding pigs and was so hungry that even the pig's food began to look good to him. He finally came to his senses and realized his father's servants fared better than him. So, he decided to go home to his father, confess he was no longer worthy to be his son, and ask for a job as a hired servant.

All the time he was gone the father never forgot about his youngest son. While he was still a long way off, the father saw him, and filled with love and compassion, he ran to meet him. Immediately he embraced and kissed his son. While the son was confessing his unworthiness to the father, the father called servants to bring a new robe for his son, as well as sandals for his feet and a ring for his finger. He told them to kill the calf they had been fattening and prepare a feast in celebration of his son who had come home.

Meanwhile, the older son came to the house from working in the field. When he heard the music, he asked what was going on. The servants told him his brother had come back home, and they were celebrating his safe return. Instead of going inside to join the celebration, the older son became angry, jealous and self-righteous, refusing to go into the house even when the father begged him to come inside. Even so, the father reaffirmed his love for the older brother, and assured him all he had was his. He went on to say it was only right to celebrate his brother's return because he was dead and is now alive; he was lost, but now is found.

The Lord promised through the prophet Ezekiel He will search for His lost ones who stray away, and He will bring them safely home again. He also promises to bandage their wounds and strengthen the weak. (Ezek. 34:16) God is looking for sons and daughters filled with His heart of compassion – those who will search for His lost ones and bring them safely home through intercession as well as by stopping for the one He places in front of them. He is also looking for church bodies who will welcome the lost ones home with a spirit of rejoicing rather than with self-righteousness and condemnation. Join the Spirit of God in calling them forth.

PRAYER

In the name of Jesus Christ, we call out to the prodigals, "Come home." In the name of Jesus Christ, we declare your eyes will be opened, and sons and daughters will come home in repentance to receive the unconditional love of the Father. We further declare, upon coming home, you will be about the family business – bringing Heaven to earth, bringing honor and glory to the Lord Jesus Christ.

In the name of Jesus Christ, we call out to the Church, "Rise up!" Rise up with the love and compassion of the Father. Rise up with a heart of intercession, which perseveres and remains watchful, filled with expectation for children to return. Rise up with arms open wide to embrace and celebrate sons and daughters coming back home safely. Rise up with words and actions of affirmation, which reflect the love of the Father who gives each one a robe of righteousness, a new identity, and sandals for washed feet. Amen.

(The following is a guide that can be used in praying for and declaring the Word over sons and daughters by name. Fill in the blanks with the name of the son or daughter you are calling home.)

Father, I thank you for _____. I thank you for their faith in you, which was once confessed and evident, and I declare your Word, no weapon formed against him/her will prosper and none of your purposes for him/her will be thwarted. (Is. 54:17; Job 42:2)

Father, I pray my heart will be turned toward _____, to bless him/her and not curse. Fill me with your love so I love _____ unconditionally as you do.

Father, open _____'s eyes to see your wonderful kindness, goodness and patience so he/she quickly turns back to you in wholehearted repentance. (Rom. 2:4)

I thank you for working in _____, and giving him/her the desire and the power to do what pleases you. (Phil. 2:13)

I declare that _____ is your sheep and he/she listens to your voice. I thank you that he/she has eternal life, and he/she will never perish because no one can snatch him/her from you. (Jn. 10:27-29)

I further declare your Word, you began a good work in _____ and you will continue your work in him/her until it is finally finished on the day when Christ Jesus returns. (Phil. 1:6)

I thank you for watching over your Word to perform it and that you do not fail to keep even one of your promises. (Jer. 1:12; Josh. 21:45) To you be glory now and forever. Amen.

LOVED, ACCEPTED AND BLESSED

Jesus Blesses Children

Matthew 19:13-15; Mark 10:13-16; Luke 18:15-17

When Jesus was in Capernaum, His disciples came to Him asking who was the greatest in the Kingdom of Heaven. In response, Jesus called a little child to Himself and placed the child in their midst. Then Jesus told them, unless they turned from their sins and became like little children, they would never get into the Kingdom of Heaven. He added, the greatest in the Kingdom of Heaven is anyone who becomes as humble as the little child placed before them.

Jesus went on to say, "And anyone who welcomes a little child like this on my behalf is welcoming me." (Matt. 18:5) But it would seem, like many today, the disciples did not "get it." For in the very next chapter of Matthew, we read parents brought their children to Jesus so He could lay His hands on them, pray for them and bless them; however, the disciples scolded the parents for "bothering" Jesus.

Jesus corrected the disciples saying, "Let the children come to me. Don't stop them! For the Kingdom of God belongs to those who are like these children." (Mark 10:14) Then taking them in His arms, Jesus placed His hands on their heads, and blessed them.

The Lord is looking in this generation for parents, godparents, grandparents, aunts, uncles and neighbors who will welcome Him by welcoming the children. Today in America children are starving spiritually. Could He have had this generation of children in mind when He penned over two thousand years ago through the prophet Jeremiah, "Rise during the night, and cry out. Pour out your hearts like water to the Lord. Lift up your hands to him in prayer, pleading for your children, for in every street they are faint with hunger." (Lam. 2:19) The Lord is looking in this generation for those who will teach the children the Word of God and how to walk in the power of the Holy Spirit, leading by example. Join the Spirit of God in calling them forth.

PRAYER

In the name of Jesus Christ, we call out to pastors, teachers, parents, godparents, grandparents, aunts, uncles and neighbors, "Bring the children to Jesus. Don't withhold from them the nourishment, which is essential for their spiritual health and well-being." In the name of Jesus Christ, we declare children are the greatest in the Kingdom of God and as such, ministering to them must be considered a privilege as well as a high priority in the Church.

To those of you who have been undervalued as children, who have suffered rejection and abandonment, we call you to be loved, accepted and blessed by the Father. In the name of Jesus Christ, we break off all rejection, and in the name of Jesus Christ, we release the Spirit of love and acceptance in the Beloved. We declare each of you has revelation of your priceless value to God – highly treasured, highly favored – so you can easily step into the destiny the Lord has for you. To Him be all glory and praise! Amen.

EXTRAVAGANT WORSHIP LEADERS

Children in the Temple

Matthew 21:12-16

After Jesus' triumphal entry into the city of Jerusalem, He entered the Temple, a house of prayer. However, the vendors who bought and sold animals for sacrifice made it more like a den of thieves than a place of prayer. Jesus overthrew the tables and drove them all out.

As He entered the Temple, those who were blind and lame came to Him and He healed them. It was the children who were heard shouting, "Praise God for the Son of David." The leaders were indignant at what the children were saying and confronted Jesus about it. He replied, "Haven't you ever read the Scriptures? For they say, 'You have taught children and infants to give you praise.'" (Matt. 21:16)

In no way, am I an authority on music. My voice is ... well, let's just say I make a joyful noise to the Lord, and He loves it. He has to. But this I know, every generation has its sound, the music it is best noted for, and it comes through the youth. The same is true in Christian music.

Growing up, most churches used organ and piano accompaniment to the hymns. With the Charismatic movement, a new sound came through Maranatha Music in the form of songs and choruses. Pipe organs gave way to guitars and drums. Today a new sound of worship is coming out of Hillsong in Australia, Jesus Culture and Bethel Music in northern California, as well as others.

It is the sound of intimacy. It is the sound of sons and daughters declaring in their music who the Lord is and what He is like. It is the sound of the bride worshipping and praising her Bridegroom in extravagant worship, not being distracted by time, but rather lavishing love upon the One who is worthy. The Lord is looking in this generation for such musicians who will receive the fresh, new songs from His Presence and lead others into intimacy with Him. Join the Spirit of God in calling them forth.

PRAYER

In the name of the Beloved, we call out to the musicians and worship leaders, "Come forth!" Come forth and spend each and every waking moment as an act of worship to the Lord so His heart becomes your heart, and your desires become His desires. Soak in His Presence. Linger with Him. Play your instruments to Him and for Him alone.

Receive from Him the new songs that delight His heart. And we declare as you receive from Him, you will be strengthened and transformed by His power and might. Then you will draw others into His Presence so the sounds of Heaven come to earth and the supernatural becomes natural. In Jesus' mighty name, amen.

DAY 28

INTERCESSORS WITH POWER AND EXPECTATION
Rhoda
Acts 12:1-17

After Pentecost, as the number of believers in Jesus Christ grew, so did the level of persecution. Herod Agrippa, king of Judea, ordered James, the brother of John, killed with a sword. He ordered Peter arrested and put in prison during the Passover celebration with 16 soldiers assigned to guard him. Herod intended to put Peter on trial after Passover. While Peter was in prison, the church gathered to pray earnestly for him.

As the church prayed, Peter was sleeping, fastened with chains between two soldiers. Suddenly an angel came and miraculously rescued him from prison. When he realized he was not dreaming but was actually free, he went to the home where they were gathered in prayer and knocked on the door. Rhoda, a servant girl, went to open the door. When she heard Peter's voice and recognized him, she got so excited she forgot to open the door. When she announced Peter was at the door, they told her she was crazy. When she persisted, they said it must be his angel!

How is it they had such low expectations when they prayed? Could it be they were praying out of fear rather than

85

out of faith? Could it be they were praying the problem instead of praying and declaring the solution? Could it be they rejected the message of a child because they forgot Jesus' words, "of such is the Kingdom of Heaven?" Could it be since James had been killed, they wondered if it was God's will for Peter to die as well? Did they forget those who come to God, must believe He is a rewarder of those who diligently seek Him? Did they forget Jesus' words, it is the devil who comes to steal, kill and destroy (John 10:10), not God? Given the circumstances, any of this is possible. However, God is looking for a generation of intercessors who are firm in their convictions that God is the Giver, and Satan is the taker. He is looking for believers who know their God and His character so they can partner with Him to bring Heaven to earth. Join the Spirit of God in calling them forth.

PRAYER

In the name of Jesus Christ, we call forth intercessors who will pray with the power of the Holy Spirit in perseverance and expectation. We call forth those who know God, know His character, hear His voice and pray His heart. We call forth those with special gifts of faith to move mountains as well as to bring Heaven to earth.

We declare as you pray in faith and declare His Word, those who are being persecuted for their faith will be strengthened, encouraged and rescued from their captors.

We declare because you have the compassion and mercy of Christ, you will take no delight in the death of the wicked;

rather, you will delight with the Father when the wicked turn from their evil ways and live.

In the name of Jesus Christ, we release the Spirit of Sōzō (salvation, healing, and deliverance) to those who do wicked and evil, bringing them to belief in Jesus Christ. We pray for al Qaeda, for Isis, for all terrorist organizations, for those involved in human trafficking as well as all who oppose the Gospel of Christ that they will have Damascus Road experiences. We declare even while they are on their way to do harm, they will be arrested by the Lord and their lives will be totally changed by His mercy and power. We declare once saved, they will have an even greater level of passion and commitment for the Lord and the expansion of His Kingdom. In the powerful name of Jesus Christ, our Lord, amen.

WAKE UP!

Eutychus
Acts 20:7-12

For those of you not familiar with the name Eutychus, he was the young man in the Bible who fell asleep during church. He may have been the first person to fall asleep in church, but he certainly won't be the last! However, don't be critical of Eutychus; there were extenuating circumstances. The church was meeting in an upstairs room, which was lit with many flickering lamps. Eutychus was sitting on the windowsill, and as Paul preached on and on until midnight, Eutychus became drowsy and fell to his death three stories below. Quite a penalty for falling asleep in church!

Paul immediately went downstairs and picked him up in his arms saying, "Don't worry; he's alive!" (Acts 20:10) Then they had the Lord's Supper, ate together, and Paul continued talking to them until dawn! In the meantime, they took the boy home alive and well.

Picture the following in your mind. The church has come together to share in the Lord's Supper and a meal. Paul, the missionary, is going to be speaking. There are so many people crowded in the room that one young man sits on the windowsill – not the most comfortable of seats. And he sits there for hours. The church was hungry to hear the Word of God. They were so hungry, in fact, they spent the entire night listening to Paul speak. Is this a picture of your church?

From what I am reading and hearing from many respected Christian voices in America, the western church for the most part is sleeping. She isn't sleeping because of meetings running well into the night or until dawn; rather, she is sleeping because of apathy, compromise, indifference and lack of life. Could it be the letter to the church in Sardis is appropriate for us too? "I know all the things you do, and that you have a reputation for being alive – but you are dead. Wake up! Strengthen what little remains, for even what is left is almost dead. I find that your actions do not meet the requirements of my God. Go back to what you heard and believed at first; hold to it firmly. Repent and turn to me again. If you don't wake up, I will come to you suddenly, as unexpected as a thief." (Rev. 3:1b-3) Join the Spirit of God in calling out to His people, "Wake up!"

PRAYER

In the name of Jesus Christ, we cry out to the church in America, "Wake up! Return to the Lord your God in humility and repentance, and be healed. Reclaim the Word of God, which has been snatched away from your hearts by the evil one. Cast your worries, cares and burdens on the Lord so you may find rest for your souls. "Draw near to Him, and He will draw near to you." (Jam. 4:8 NKJV) Make your heart His, wholly His, so you are a part of the beautiful bride He is returning for – a bride without spot, wrinkle or blemish. (Eph. 5:27) Amen.

MENTORED TO LEAD BY EXAMPLE
Timothy
Acts 16:1-5 and 2 Timothy 1:5-7

Timothy (Greek: meaning *honoring God* or *honored by God*) is first introduced in Acts 16 during Paul's second missionary journey. Timothy is mentioned as a "young disciple," living in Lystra. His mother and grandmother were Jewish believers, but his father was Greek (not Jewish). There is no indication in Scripture that his father was a believer. Timothy was taught the Scriptures from childhood (2 Tim. 3:15) and was well thought of by the believers in Lystra. (Acts 16:2) So Paul wanted Timothy to join him and Silas on their journey.

Paul steps up to become a spiritual father to Timothy, addressing him as, "my true son in the faith" (1 Tim. 1:2) and "my dear son." (2 Tim. 1:2) In his first letter to Timothy, Paul encourages him saying, "Don't let anyone think less of you because you are young. Be an example to all believers in what you say, in the way you live, in your love, your faith, and your purity." (1 Tim. 4:12)

In Romans 16, Paul calls Timothy his "fellow worker" (vs. 21), and he entrusted him with missions of great importance. Paul wrote to the Philippians about Timothy saying,

"I have no one like him." (Phil. 2:20) Timothy was imprisoned at least once for his faith as Hebrews states, "our brother Timothy has been released from jail." (Heb. 13:23)

Timothy came to faith as a child, and he finished well. God is looking in this generation for those, like Timothy, who are willing to humbly submit themselves to mentorship. He is also looking for those like Paul – faithful men and women of God, filled with the Holy Spirit and power – willing to invest in the lives of the generation after them through mentorship. We frequently say we need the Lord to send laborers into His harvest field. While that may be true, perhaps we are overlooking the laborers He has already sent because we are ignoring the younger generation behind us. Join the Spirit of God in calling forth the mentors and mentees in this generation.

PRAYER

In the name of Jesus Christ, we call out to men and women of God, mature in the Lord, filled with the Holy Spirit and with His power, "Step up! Step up to mentor the young in the faith coming behind you."

We declare you have eyes to see those like Timothy, who will be a blessing not only to you, but to the body of Christ as well. We declare you will find delight in your ceiling becoming their floor. We further declare when the time is right, you will release them to partner with God in bringing His Kingdom to earth.

In the name of Jesus Christ, we call out to young laid down lovers of God, willing to submit to Godly authority and mentorship, "Come forth!" We declare as you are mentored by those filled with the Holy Spirit and His power, the treasure planted within you before the foundation of the world will surface as pure gold. We further declare you will not fail, and like Timothy, you will finish well, faithful to the end. Amen.

CALLED TO BE THE BRIDE
Sons and Daughters

The last words of Jesus recorded in the Bible are, "Yes, I am coming soon!" (Rev. 22:20) He is returning for His beautiful bride clothed in purity, wearing a gown of righteousness that He so generously and sacrificially provided. She eagerly anticipates His return because she now has an intimacy with Him that for years she only dreamed of having. How she longs to see her Beloved face to face.

Even now, her heart fills with joy every time He draws near. His fragrance is so sweet to her nostrils. She delights in His love and hangs on His every word. It seems almost unbelievable that He wrote the words to her, "I have loved you with an everlasting love; therefore with lovingkindness I have drawn you." (Jer. 31:3 NKJV) He beckons to her, and she quickly responds. She will leave anything to be with Him, for there is nothing that compares to His Presence and wraparound love. Even when they are apart, her every thought is of Him and how she might bring Him a measure of the delight that He has given to her. Everything she does, no matter how great or how seemingly insignificant, she does as an act of worship for Him.

No one can be around her long without hearing about her Bridegroom. She longs for everyone to know Him and the forgiveness, joy and freedom she has found in Him. She will take risk and do anything that He asks of her so that He receives all He died for. He is her Beloved, and she is His bride.

This is a picture of the bride that Jesus is looking for. He is not looking for those who attend church and serve Him because it is the right thing to do or out of a sense of duty. He is not interested in Christian disciplines although they can be helpful in drawing near to Him. He is looking for sons and daughters who will become laid down lovers, who will give Him a home in their hearts – a home for Him alone. He is looking for intimacy, those who are willing to get carried away in His love and in His Presence. And He is looking for those who will take up risk to bring Heaven to earth by loving their neighbor one person at a time. Will you be His bride? If your answer is, "Yes," then pour out your heart to Jesus, your Beloved, in surrender, love and adoration. He is waiting for you. Take time to soak in His Presence.

MY PRAYER

EPILOGUE

On April 28, 2015 when praying for this generation, I was fully awake, but had my eyes closed. Suddenly a vision appeared before me. I saw a huge banquet hall without walls; it seemed endless. The room was filled with long banquet tables positioned around the hall as far as I could see. While I was aware the tables were filled, I did not notice what was on them; rather, I was in complete awe of the immense vastness of this banquet hall, which was without borders.

Then a Voice spoke saying, "The banquet is ready. Call forth the poor, the lame, the halt and the blind." There was an urgent tone from the One speaking as if He were saying, "Time is running out!" Later I looked up the passage of Scripture quoted, Luke 14:15-24 (KJV); it is the parable Jesus told of the Great Feast.

Not certain what "the halt" meant, I searched out the meanings of the poor, the lame, the halt, and the blind. The poor, while including the beggar, is certainly not limited to the poor and homeless. Rather, it also encompasses the lowly, the helpless, the powerless, the needy, and those destitute of learning. Isn't that certainly a description of the children of today?

The lame is used to describe the disabled, crippled, and injured. This, too, is a picture of the generation of today, many of whom attend public schools where God, prayer and the Bible have been removed.

The halt means to be missing a limb – particularly, a foot, which speaks to the sure foundation of Christianity having been taken away from the training of our children.

The blind speaks of their condition spiritually. It speaks for itself.

I came away from His Presence shaken at the gravity of their condition. However, with the shaking came expectant hope, for our loving and merciful Father has given the solution. We must intercede for the children of this generation, contending for, as well as calling forth God's heart for them.

Now is the time for your response. Will you be like Abram and Sarai, who in unbelief, ignored God's instruction and, instead, came up with a deficient plan? Or will you be like Abraham and Sarah and, by faith and obedience, accept His call to father and mother this generation? The choice is up to you! Will you join the Spirit and the bride in contending for, proclaiming and calling forth God's heart for the children?